PLEASE KEEP THIS
BOOK CLEAN

D0108458

CHAMPION OF ARBOR DAY:
J. Sterling Morton

Champion of Arbor Day: J. Sterling Morton is part of THE
GREAT HEARTLANDERS SERIES. This collection
of biographies for children describes the lives of local
heroes — men and women of all races and careers —
who have made a lasting contribution to the nation and
the world.

CHAMPION OF ARBOR DAY: J. Sterling Morton

Copyright © 1998 by Acorn Books

Acorn Books
7337 Terrace
Kansas City, MO 64114

Library of Congress Cataloguing-in-Publication Data
Beaty, Sandy and J.L. Wilkerson
          Champion of Arbor Day / by Sandy Beaty and J. L.
Wilkerson
          Library of Congress Catalog Card Number: 98-071418
          Series Title: The Great Heartlanders Series
ISBN 0-9664470-1-8
1. J. Sterling Morton, 1832-1902 - Juvenile literature. 2. Nebraska - Biography - History - Juvenile literature.

10 9 8 7 6 5 4 3 2 1

Dedication:

For all the friends and supporters of
THE GREAT HEARTLANDERS SERIES
who understand the importance of providing children
the opportunity to learn about their local heroes.

Acknowledgments:

Special thanks to Betty Dixon and Shirley Rapp for
their careful attention to detail.
Chad Wall, Nebraska State Historical Society, for his
painstaking efforts in providing many of the outstanding
images in this book.

Cover Design and Book Layout/Design:
Shirley Harryman, Stonehouse Studio of Kansas City,
Missouri

Photo Credits:
Nebraska State Historical Society, pages 5, 10, 33, 43,
57, 63, 77, 88, 89, 97, 102, 123, 128 and 129.
Alexander Majors Historical Trust, page 71.

In celebration of the first Arbor Day in 1872, J. Sterling Morton wrote an article for the *Omaha Daily Herald*. He said:

May it become a joy forever... May all the people strive on that day to plant... many, many trees, both forest and fruit. May the day and the observance thereof be cherished in every household in the state forever, and its name and fruits become as a shower of blessings to the long lines of generations who shall succeed us in the short, quick trip which all humanity must make, from the cradle to the grave.

Contents

The Nest

It was one of his earliest memories.

The room was almost dark. Heavy curtains draped the long windows. At the far end of the room, several people gathered around a bed. They spoke to each other in hushed, worried tones as they stared at the sick woman lying there.

The woman's hair was a brilliant red. The long curls fell over the white pillow like a thousand rose petals.

The year was 1840. J. Sterling Morton was only eight years old, but he would always remember that image: the white pillow and his Aunt Mary's red, red hair. In the dark room, they seemed the only source of brightness.

Sterling stepped toward one of the windows. The curtains were parted slightly, and a slender wedge of light shone through. Inside was a sick-room, but outside was a warm spring day. The sweet smell of lilacs floated through the parted curtains. Robins twittered in a nearby tree. Sterling longed to be outside.

Sterling's cousin shook his arm. "What's happening now?" he whispered, and pointed toward the bed.

The doctor, a short man with a bushy white beard, put his hand on Aunt Mary's forehead. He frowned. Then he reached inside his leather bag and pulled out long, sharp-pointed scissors. He leaned over Aunt Mary's head. Two women standing by the bed began to cry softly.

"What's he doing?" Sterling's cousin asked.

"They say if you're sick with a high fever," Sterling explained, "sometimes cutting off your hair will make you better."

The doctor grabbed a handful of the red hair. Snip, snip, snip went the scissors blades. In huge mounds, the blazing red hair dropped to the floor.

After he cut the hair, someone swept it into a corner. Everyone stared at Aunt Mary in hopes of seeing some immediate change in her condition. No one noticed Sterling slip across the room and pick up Aunt Mary's hair.

Sterling tiptoed from the room and headed toward the front door.

They were still there! Two robins hopped over the ground near the porch. They were searching for good nesting material. Sterling had watched them for two days. The birds had made a poor start, using a few sticks and twigs they found scattered on the ground, but they were a long way from finishing their little home.

Slowly, gently, Sterling stretched out his arms and laid Aunt Mary's hair on the grass. Then, just as slowly, he backed away.

The robins cautiously approached the hair. They circled the red mound, chirping to each other. Sterling had to stop himself from laughing. He felt he could read their minds: "Do we dare?" "Is it a trick?" they seemed to be asking. Sterling wanted to call out, "It's all right. It won't hurt you!" But he knew he had to remain motionless and patient.

In a few minutes the two birds dragged away some of the silky strands. And then, with their wings beating hard against the weight, they flew to their nest in a nearby pine tree. Sterling watched as the birds darted back and forth from hair to tree.

Soon the nest began to take shape. Cradled

in the long graceful branches of the pine tree, the bird's home looked like a ball of fiery red yarn. Only when one of the robins settled into the finished nest, stitched together with Aunt Mary's red hair, did Sterling finally tiptoe back inside the house.

As weeks went by and Aunt Mary's health improved, her family began to talk about her hair. At that time it was unfashionable for women to have short hair. And so plans were made for Aunt Mary to wear a wig until her hair grew out. Wigmakers, however, needed her hair to create the wig.

But where was Aunt Mary's hair?

A great hunt began for the missing locks. Under the bed. In the dust-bin. Behind all the doors. Rooms were searched again and again, and still no brilliant red hair. It should be so easy to find, but no one had any luck.

During the search, Sterling hid in a maple tree. He felt so guilty. It never occurred to him that anyone would ever want the hair. Finally, when he saw his mother standing on the porch alone, he jumped out of the tree and ran to her.

He slipped his hand into hers, and pulled her down so she could hear him whisper, "I gave it to the birds. Aunt Mary's hair. I gave it to the robins."

"You did what?" his mother exclaimed. "To

Julius Sterling Morton's middle name came from his mother. Emeline Morton's maiden name was Sterling. This is a painting of her as a young woman.

the robins? Why on earth would you do that?"

"They needed it for their nest," he said. "I didn't know Aunt Mary would want her hair again." When his mother didn't say anything, he added, "I didn't mean to do anything wrong."

Emeline Morton kissed the top of her son's head. "Making a home is more important than making a wig, Sterling. Your Aunt Mary will be proud of you — that was a clever and kind thing to do."

When his mother told the others about the hair and nest, everyone rushed outside.

"Where's this architectural wonder?" asked Uncle Edward. Edward Morton, Sterling's favorite uncle, loved to tease his nephew. The boy spent almost every afternoon at Uncle Edward's office where he ran the town's newspaper. "Sounds to me as if this nest caper is newsworthy enough for the front page of *The Monroe Advocate*."

Everyone looked up at the pine tree. The nest's merry color made it easy to spot. All the grown-ups laughed. "Isn't that just like Sterling?" someone said. They all agreed helping birds build a nest — anything involving nature — was typical of J. Sterling Morton.

"If he's not hovering around the *Advocate* presses," said Uncle Edward, with a wink at Sterling, "he's off on a hike through the woods."

Sterling smiled. His family was right. Newspapers and nature — his great loves. Sterling was happy that he wasn't in trouble for giving away Aunt Mary's hair. But he was especially glad that the robins were snug and safe.

Months later, when the robins had moved on, Uncle Edward climbed up the pine tree at Emeline's request and brought down the remarkable nest. Through the years, Sterling's family would look at the nest and tell the story over and over. It became a family "trophy," and a fitting piece of history in the life of J. Sterling Morton, champion of Arbor Day.

A New Life

The day was warm and sunny. Wagons and buggies lined the dirt road which ran by the river. The horses grazed on little tufts of grass in the middle of the road or dozed where they stood.

A group of men and women waded in the shallows of the river. Pants and skirts were lifted modestly above the swirling water.

One of the men, a preacher, held up a baby and announced, "From the union of Julius Dewey Morton and Emeline Sterling Morton has come this new life, a son. He entered the world on April 22 in the year 1832 in Adams, New York."

The preacher then dipped the baby into the river. The baby wailed when he felt the cold water.

Trying to speak over the clamoring infant, the

9

In 1832, J. Sterling Morton was born in this house in Adams, New York. Within three years of his birth, his family moved to Monroe, Michigan, a bustling community on the edge of the American West.

minister shouted, "And he shall be called Julius Sterling Morton."

Despite the formal ceremony and the solemn words, Sterling's parents could barely keep from laughing.

"I believe you could hear him in all 24 states!" bragged Julius, as the family rode away in the buggy afterwards.

"Maybe he cried because he's so little for such a big name," Emeline said, and laughed.

Julius' father, Abner, lifted the baby from Emeline's lap and set Sterling on his knee. "He'll grow into his name," he said.

As they rode along, the family wondered aloud what the future might hold for the tiny boy.

"He'll probably end up with black ink on his hands and face, like you and Edward," Julius said to his father. "Seems like newspaper publishing is in the Morton blood."

"He could do worse," said Abner. "Of course, newspaper work got me in trouble a time or two," he added with a chuckle. Abner was an outspoken man. He had strong political opinions — sometimes unpopular opinions — which he stubbornly insisted on expressing in his newspaper. "Speak your mind!" That was Grandfather Abner's motto. Many years later, when J. Sterling Morton became a newspaperman, his critics would complain that the grand-son was just like his grandfather — outspoken and stubborn.

"He might want to be a merchant like you, Julius," Abner said.

Sterling's little head drooped forward. He was asleep.

"Look at that," said Emeline and smiled. "We've tired him out from all these occupations we're planning for him."

Abner handed the sleeping infant to his mother. "Whatever he sets his mind to do, he'll

want to look beyond Adams, New York," said
Abner. "The country is growing, just like this
family. I've been thinking maybe I'll pack up the
press and head out west. I've heard some
promising things about Michigan."

Julius and Emeline looked at each other.
Abner was 67 years old. Was he seriously thinking about leaving New York and traveling into
the Northwest Territory? Although several
states had already been carved out of the territory — Ohio, Indiana and Illinois — the country
was still a wilderness. Didn't Abner know that
life out west was full of dangers, even for men
half his age?

But Abner was certainly a stubborn man.
Two years later, Grandfather Morton was on his
way to Michigan. And that's not all. He convinced Julius and Emeline to join him. On the
frontier a person could start a new life.

"Anything — everything! — is possible out
west," Julius told Emeline. "A person can make
a real contribution out there, do something to
make a difference in the world." He looked at
his son, Sterling, playing in the front yard.
"Father's right. The country is moving west.
That's the best place to raise our family."

The Mortons traveled west on a boat down
the Erie Canal. The recently completed waterway connected eastern New York with Lake

Erie. From the canal they boarded a boat on Lake Erie, which took them to Monroe in southeast Michigan.

The family chose Monroe because it was a busy crossroads. With 1,600 people, it was as big as another growing town to the west, Chicago on Lake Michigan. Mail stages and lake traffic used Monroe as a jumping off place for lands farther west. Here traders stocked up on goods and supplies, and pioneer families began their search for a place on the frontier to call their own. Native Americans also lived in the territory and traded furs for sugar and flour in Monroe.

Abner set up his press and soon began publishing his newspaper. Before long, Edward Morton joined him. Now all the Morton men and their families were in Monroe. As business grew, Abner was glad to have Edward's help. Together they bought out the only rival newspaper in town and merged both papers into the *Monroe Advocate*.

Julius ran a trading business. He bought and sold commodities. For example, Julius would sometimes advertise that he needed 1,000 pounds of butter or 5,000 bushels of rye or some other commodity which he would trade for cash or other goods.

People admired Julius for both his good business sense and his honesty. When he was a boy in New York, Julius worked as a clerk for an elderly man named Mr. W. P. McKinstry who ran a general store. Later, when Mr. McKinstry was about to die, he asked to see Julius, a teenager at the time. Mr. McKinstry so trusted the boy's honesty and skill that he wanted Julius, instead of older, professional men, to settle his business affairs before he died.

The Morton family prospered in Monroe. The family also grew. William and Emma were born to Julius and Emeline within a few years after the Mortons arrived in Michigan. As Julius became more and more respected in the community, he was determined to see that his children had every opportunity to succeed. And Julius had some very definite ideas about how to succeed.

"Thrift. Independence. Piety," Julius announced to his children one day. "You must make a contribution to your community."

Dressed in their best Sunday clothes, Sterling, William and Emma sat in a row on the sofa. They had heard this speech before.

"Those qualities will carry you far," Julius said.

William and Emma nodded attentively at their father. Only Sterling seemed distracted. He tugged at his over-sized collar. He stared at his nose by crossing his eyes. He leaned over to pat the cat.

"Sterling," said Julius, "what is piety?"

Sterling scratched the cat's head as it rubbed its back across his dangling leg. "Piety is dutiful conduct," he answered.

"Very good," said his father. "And what is dutiful conduct?"

Sterling thought for a moment. "Hard work," he said.

Julius wasn't sure whether Sterling was making a joke or not. Piety was something Sterling had a difficult time practicing. As a prank, Sterling had once thrown the cat onto the back of unsuspecting Uncle Edward — while the family knelt in prayer!

Julius and Emeline tended to spoil their son because he was exceptionally smart. This only encouraged his mischievous habits. When he was an adult, Sterling admitted that as a child he was accustomed to getting his own way. "I was remarkable for willfulness," said Sterling. Nevertheless, the bright and friendly Sterling was well-liked.

Julius and Emeline worried about their son's willfulness. But they needn't have. In years to come, the lessons Sterling learned from his family would, as his father said, "carry him far." He would "speak his own mind." He would "make a contribution." And when he ran up against resistance to his ideas — ideas like Arbor Day — a little determination to "get his own way" turned out to be a very good quality, indeed.

Coming & Going

Steamboats navigated Lake Erie. Caravans of wagons rolled along the dusty roads of the town. It seemed to 14-year-old Sterling that everyone was going somewhere. Everyone but Sterling. His town of Monroe, Michigan, was just a place to pass through!

As he watched, Sterling tried to estimate the number of travelers and decided there must be more immigrants in the boats and wagons than all the residents in Monroe added together! Maybe someday he would be one of the travelers, off to explore the frontier beyond his hometown. Michigan was no longer a territory. It became a state in 1837. Maybe Sterling would set out for one of the new western territories, as his grandfather and parents did when they left New York.

Sterling climbed a tree near Lake Erie's shore

where he could watch the ships dock at the harbor. Freight and passengers filled the crowded boats. Some of the passengers were immigrants. A few of them debarked at Monroe. Their possessions were brought out of the ship's hold and stacked on shore.

Sterling was always interested in seeing all the goods people brought with them. Most household items looked alike. Every home had candle molds, because everyone needed the light which candles provided. A butter churn was also a necessity, because butter was made fresh at home. Every fireplace had a flatiron near it, to be heated for pressing clothes and linens. Spinning wheels and looms made yarn and fabric.

When the house was in order, the children in a new family began to attend school. The *American Spelling Book* was filled with reading and writing lessons for all ages. It had been written by Noah Webster, and was commonly called the "blue-backed speller." *Pike's Arithmetic* was the only book available for learning to solve number problems.

Before long Sterling had mastered his textbooks. Even though he was easily distracted from his

Butter churn

studies, Sterling was a quick learner. Math problems like these from *Pike's* were simple for him:

Said Jack to Harry, 'You have only 77 chest nuts, but I have seven times as many. How many have I?'

Eighty men shared equally in a prize and received 17 dollars each. How much was the prize?

If a man was 75 years old in the year 1821, in what year was he born?

Every day when school let out, Sterling went immediately to Uncle Edward's newspaper office to find out what was happening in the world beyond Monroe. At the *Monroe Advocate*, he enjoyed reading about other countries, and about the way the United States was growing and changing. Sterling also loved to hear his uncle talk about the news.

Like other people who ran newspapers in the 1800s, Edward used his paper to print controversial political articles. He always expressed his own opinions. He praised his friends wildly, and he railed against his enemies. Sometimes people — friend and foe — would drop by the newspaper office to debate with Edward. The conversation was always lively. One time a man walked into the office and angrily threw the *Advocate* on the floor.

"Pack of lies," said the man, "and them that tells 'em is a liar." The man stared hard at Uncle

Edward.

Uncle Edward had written an article supporting James K. Polk, a Tennessee Democrat running for U.S. President. Polk was an expansionist. Like many Americans, he believed that it was the destiny of the United States to own all the land between the Atlantic Ocean and the Pacific Ocean. Polk and others encouraged immigrants to settle the far western frontiers. At that time, Mexico owned much of the western frontier which today is California, Nevada, Utah, Arizona, New Mexico, Texas and parts of Colorado and Wyoming. Polk wanted to go to war to capture the Mexican land for United States immigrants.

"Manifest Destiny!" shouted Uncle Edward. "It's our right and duty to open up the west for settlement. And any scalawag who says differently is un-American."

"James Polk's a greedy, land-grabbin' warmonger," said the man.

"Land-grabbing? What do you call us here in Michigan?" countered Uncle Edward. "The land you're standing on was once Indian Territory."

"We bought it, free and clear," said the man.

"I beg to differ, sir," said Edward. "We just plain took it."

Back and forth the argument went. Finally it ended, like most arguments at the *Advocate*, with an invitation to eat supper at the tavern next door.

Sterling learned as much about politics by listening to debates at the *Advocate* as he learned in school. Mostly Sterling learned by asking questions. And he was full of questions for his Uncle Edward. How did the U.S. acquire Michigan and all the other territories? What's "Manifest Destiny?" Why were there different political parties?

Sterling was lucky. His uncle patiently answered his questions and, at home, his parents encouraged his inquisitive mind. Although Sterling did well at the Monroe school, that inquisitive mind often got him into trouble. Having listened to heated discussions at the *Advocate*, Sterling sometimes practiced his own debating skills at school. His disapproving teacher would complain to Julius and Emeline. The teacher also pointed out that instead of sitting at his desk on school days Sterling was sometimes down by the harbor watching the boats arrive.

The Mortons wondered what they should do about this mischievous son. Sterling had long since learned the lessons from Webster's "blue-backed speller" and *Pike's Arithmetic*. Julius and Emeline talked seriously of sending Sterling to a school outside Monroe.

One evening Uncle Edward came for dinner. Afterwards, he and Sterling sat outside on the front porch, talking about what the boy would do the next year.

"I don't need to go to school," Sterling said flatly. He hoped Edward would talk his parents out of sending him away to school. "I can learn everything I need to know down at the newspaper, with you and Granddad Abner."

"You're a smart boy, Sterling," Edward said, "and what's more, you're a good boy, in spite of your mischief. But sometimes you don't think before you speak."

"I don't see what I did wrong at school," said Morton, embarrassed at his uncle's scolding. "I was just debating. The teacher said I shouldn't call somebody a 'scalawag' and a `greedy, land-grabbing warmonger'."

Edward shook his head. "School isn't the same as a newspaper office."

"But you've always told me to say what I think. Not to be lukewarm in my convictions. You've said I shouldn't let others change my mind when I know I'm right."

"Calling people bad names isn't the same thing as having convictions.

"You call people names," Sterling said.

Uncle Edward cleared his throat and shifted uneasily in his chair. "You're right," he admitted.

"I don't always do the smart thing. I'm just telling you to think before you speak. That's not just the polite thing to do, it's also the smart thing. You have to decide for yourself what you believe in and not just repeat things you hear down at the *Advocate*."

When Edward went back inside to rejoin the rest of the Mortons, Sterling stayed behind. He knew they were all talking about him. Although he heard their hushed voices, Sterling couldn't make out exactly what they were saying. But he knew the subject: his schooling.

Sterling leaned on the porch railing and stared at the forest across the road. Like a giant glowing ember, the setting sun hovered just over the tree tops.

Why did he have to go on to school — especially a school away from Monroe? Sterling was confident Uncle Edward would talk his parents out of sending him to school. After all, Edward only attended school for a year before he was apprenticed to a printer, and now he was one of the best newspapermen in the state of Michigan. Everybody said so.

Convictions? Sterling most certainly *did* have convictions. Why, he had already decided he was going to be the biggest, most important newspaperman in the entire western United States of America. Now if that wasn't conviction, he didn't know what was. In fact, he was thinking of a name for his newspaper — the *J. Sterling Morton's Great Western Advocate* — when his father stepped out on the porch. Sterling's mother, Uncle Edward and Granddad Abner followed.

"Sterling, the decision is made, " Julius announced. "You're going to Wesleyan Seminary in Albion."

J. Sterling Morton grew up in Monroe, Michigan. He attended school in Albion, Michigan.

Albion

Wesleyan Seminary! Sterling was dumb-founded. The school was advertised as an institution that would "confer a critical and thorough English education, and...give instruction both in the Ancient and Modern Languages and the General Principles of Science."

What kind of school was that for a fellow who was going to be the biggest, most important newspaperman in the entire western United States of America?

"I don't need an English education," Sterling told his parents. "I'm not some blue-blooded aristocrat. And what good is `Ancient?' Ancient is past. It's over and done with. Uncle Edward would never publish something in the *Advocate* that was ancient."

Julius and Emeline were patient. They knew Sterling was dead set against going to Wesleyan, but they were convinced that the school's well-rounded education was important for Sterling, no matter what career he chose. At Wesleyan, he would study ancient and modern languages, chemistry, history, and astronomy. His parents also liked the school's strong emphasis on discipline. They knew that Sterling's lively and headstrong nature was often his worst enemy.

"Albion, Michigan is a quiet little town," Emeline explained. "It's the kind of place where you can learn without being distracted." She avoided saying, "so you won't get into trouble," but that's exactly what she and Julius hoped Wesleyan and Albion would mean for Sterling.

"Quiet? What about the rugged wilderness of the American west? That's where I plan to live," said Sterling. Monroe was becoming much too civilized, as far as Sterling was concerned. Little shops lined the main street. His mother even had one of those new inventions — a sewing machine. "I'm not interested in `quiet'," Sterling added, grandly. "Daniel Boone, Manuel Lisa, John Colter, Dave Crockett — not one of them settled for `quiet'."

"Not one of them ran a newspaper either," said Julius. "A newspaper owner in this day and age needs a thorough education."

Nevertheless, as Julius had said, "the decision is made." Sterling's parents would not change their minds about Wesleyan. With her new sewing machine, Emeline had already begun making Sterling new shirts, pants and coats for school. His father soon bought him a train ticket. Monroe had trains as early as 1840, but train trips were still rare. Consequently, despite his disappointment at having to go to school, Sterling looked forward to the 100-mile ride to Albion on the "Iron Horse," as the locomotive was called.

At the railroad station, Julius handed Sterling twenty-five cents.

"That's the fee for using the library this semester," he said. "Wesleyan has more than 600 books. And there are current magazines, too, from Boston, Cincinnati and New York. I know you don't want to go, Sterling, but I expect you to do your best and make the most out of what's there."

Sterling knew perfectly well what his father meant by "do your best." And over the next few weeks, Sterling tried hard to concentrate on his studies and to keep out of trouble. It helped that he was, as Uncle Edward said, "a smart boy." Sterling had no trouble making good grades. What he did have trouble with, though, were the school's many rules. Students were required

to rise in the morning at the ringing of the bell, sweep and adjust their rooms;

to assemble in the chapel for prayers, morning and evening, at the tolling of the appropriate bells,

to indulge in no hallooing, loud talking, running, jumping, whistling, or other disturbance, in the rooms or halls of the Seminary...

to visit no taverns, groceries, or other places, for pleasure or entertainment...

On Sundays, students were

to make no noise, or disturbance, on that day, not to go abroad into the fields or village, or to collect at each other's rooms without permission.

Sterling wrote to his family that life at Wesleyan was " just bells and rules." He lamented the tiresome restrictions and the constant "dong, dong, dong" which governed his life from dawn to dusk. Even the food was bad, he complained.

One day the school served what the students called "bad butter." The next day Sterling was called before the faculty. Someone had spread butter on an upper hall door.

"I did it," Sterling admitted immediately.

When the panel of teachers asked why, Sterling responded, "I was trying to see if the butter was strong enough to pull the handles off the door."

"Such behavior might make the other students laugh," said his father. "But it's hardly the dignified conduct of a young man who plans to be 'the biggest, most important newspaperman in the entire western United States of America'."

Sterling agreed. But he still managed to continue to get into trouble. At least for a while. And then something happened at Wesleyan which changed not only Sterling's behavior, but his life, forever.

5

Carrie

Dong! Dong! Dong! Dong! Sterling buried his head beneath his pillow. Dong! Dong! Dong! Dong!

He could *still* hear the bells! Sometimes he even dreamed of bells. Tiny, tinkling bells. And gigantic, gonging bells the size of the Liberty Bell in Philadelphia. He once dreamed that a four-legged bell was chasing him across the Wesleyan campus. He had thrashed so hard in his sleep, trying to get away from the clanging thing, that he rolled out of bed and woke up.

This morning he sat on the edge of his bed and covered his ears until the donging stopped. When it was finally silent, Sterling remembered that he was supposed to meet "The Clever Fellows." This was a group of boys who had formed a literary club, and Sterling was the president.

He quickly tidied his room, grabbed a jumbled pile of papers and raced outside. As he ran across campus the dew on the grass soaked through his trouser cuffs. A cool autumn breeze stirred the papers he carried. He pulled them close to his chest, but one slipped loose and fluttered away. When Sterling tried to reach for it, the other papers fell from his arms.

Sterling dropped to his knees and began collecting the scattered sheets, already limp from the wet grass. He muttered to himself, "I'll never make it. I'll never make it." He just knew the bells announcing chapel would start any moment before he could meet with the literary club.

All at once a slender hand reached in front of him. Sterling looked up to see a girl leaning over him.

"Need some help?" she asked, and started picking up the papers. Her dark eyes, big as buck-eyes, sparkled. She smiled. "It might be easier to hold on to them if you stacked them like this."

Sterling stared at her face as she arranged the papers until the corners were neatly aligned. This was the prettiest girl he had ever seen in his entire life. He barely noticed his knees sinking

This is J. Sterling Morton's signature. He always signed his name in the margin of page 32 of his favorite books.

32

further and further into the sodden ground. Wesleyan's star debater and president of the literary society was speechless.

"I'm Caroline," she said, and handed him the papers. She waited for him to say something, but Sterling still could do nothing but stare at her. "Caroline Joy

Caroline "Carrie" Morton was J. Sterling Morton's wife. She and Sterling dreamed of making a home on the frontier.

French," she said finally. "I'm from Detroit."

Suddenly the Wesleyan bells rang out. The sound, like a blast from the four-legged monster of his dream, brought Sterling to his senses.

"It's time for chapel," Caroline said, and started to walk away.

"Wait a minute," Sterling called after her. "I'll walk with you." He scrambled to his feet. They both looked down at the bottom of his trousers. The legs were soaked, and his knees were covered in mud. Sterling grinned. "I'll just tell them that chapel is so important that I walked on my hands and knees to get there."

Caroline laughed. The sound was so thoroughly enchanting that the other noise — those awful bells — seemed to fade away.

"I'm Julius Sterling Morton of Monroe," he said, as they walked toward chapel. "But you may call me Sterling."

"And you may call me Carrie," she said.

Fourteen-year-old Carrie was one year younger than Sterling. She was born in Maine and came to Michigan as a baby, the only child of Hiram and Caroline Joy. Soon after arriving in Detroit, Carrie's mother became very ill. Life was hard on the frontier, and Mrs. Joy worried about her baby daughter growing up with just a father. So before she died, she asked Hiram to promise that he would ask their neighbors, Deacon and Cynthia French, to act as another set of parents. The childless Frenches agreed.

⟫⟫◆⟪⟪

There is a moment in everyone's life when something happens that is so important and so remarkable that it remains in one's memory forever. Those are moments, clear and bright as stars on a cloudless night, which stay fixed in a person's mind as if they were events from only yesterday.

The meeting of Sterling and Carrie was just such a moment. Both remembered it for the rest of their lives because from that moment their lives remained intertwined.

Within a few days of their meeting, Sterling asked Carrie to marry him. She said yes. Under the towering canopy of Albion's old trees, they pledged eternal love. But they would wait. Neither wanted to marry until each had finished school. That would be seven years.

No one took the couple seriously. Seven years was a lifetime for people as young as 14 and 15. It was just a youthful infatuation, everyone said. After all, Sterling wasn't any good at waiting. He was headstrong. His impulsive nature had repeatedly caused him trouble.

It was a testament to his genuine love for Carrie that he did exactly as they planned. He waited. School never had much appeal to Sterling, but now he applied himself. He studied harder and behaved better than he ever had before. And he devoted himself to preparing for a career after school. He continued to talk of establishing a newspaper on the frontier. Naturally, when his group, Clever Fellows, decided to produce a literary magazine, Sterling was put in charge. He wrote a third of the magazine articles and was the editor for the rest.

Once or twice the temptation to change his plans was very great. In 1849, for example, Sterling decided that he must go to California. Gold had been discovered a year earlier. Already 80,000 people had dropped their jobs and obligations in the east and set out for the gold fields. Waves of fortune seekers streamed through eastern Michigan. Others traveled across Ohio, Kentucky and Tennessee. They were all dream-

ers of gold, heading west toward the trails which led to California and riches. Why should a man spend a lifetime working to make a bare-bones living when he could make a king's fortune in a few weeks?

They were called the Forty-Niners, and Sterling wanted to be one of them. His family pleaded with him not to go. Already stories were coming back from the gold fields about life in the mining camps: bloody brawls, robberies, even murders. So many people moved into the gold fields that prices for everyday goods sky-rocketed. An egg cost fifty cents. A pair of boots cost $100.

The dreams ended. Only a handful of people ever struck it rich from the Gold Rush. Most returned home empty handed or settled in the rich farmlands they had seen along the trails.

Sterling remained in Michigan. The year after the first big Gold Rush wave, he headed off to the University of Michigan in Ann Arbor. Carrie left for a girls school in Utica, New York.

As the train took him to the university, Sterling looked out the window toward the setting sun. Maybe not California, he told himself. Maybe not gold. But out there, out west some-where, he would find his own dream.

6

University of Michigan

Dreams are fine and necessary. But dreams come to nothing without diligence. Sterling knew this and, soon after arriving in Ann Arbor, he wrote his father, "My ambition to be *somebody* is slowly wakeing [sic] up and if I can only keep straight, be contented and have my health, no one knows what I may not attain to."

Sterling determined to "keep straight." He did his best, as his father had urged him four years earlier. He kept a diary where he recorded his goals — and failings.

On January 5, 1851, he wrote, "Resolved today upon turning over a new leaf in the book of my existence, and writing thereon Honesty, Industry and Stoicism. Shall I?"

A month later, disappointed with himself, he wrote, "Have lost the day, in it accomplished nothing good. Must commence a new account tomorrow morning. And I will! Shall not play checkers again in a week."

As at Wesleyan, life at the university was governed by a bell. It tolled every hour, beginning before dawn and ending shortly after dark. Its clanging awoke the students, warned them of the start and end of classes, and signaled them to put out lights at night.

For all his good intentions, Sterling managed to get into trouble from time to time. His chief target of mischief was, of course, the bell. With the entire day punctuated with clanging, Sterling and his friends decided to take radical action.

They called themselves the "Committee on Acoustics." Although acoustics is the science of sound, the purpose of the committee was to find a way to *stop* the sound of the bell.

They tried everything, but nothing worked. Morton wrote in his diary, "...efforts...thus far have proved entirely futile. That jingling old bell will ring in spite of chains, padlocks or anything which the `Committee on Acoustics' has yet found."

And then someone came up with a clever, fool-proof plan.

One winter evening, committee members sneaked outside. They tipped over the bell, holding its clacker so no one would hear them. Next they filled the upside-down bell with water. They knew the water would freeze by morning. When the janitor, who was in charge of ringing the bell, came out at dawn, "the jingling old bell" would be silent.

When committee members returned to their rooms, they could hardly contain their laughter. Should they stay up to watch the expression on the surprised janitor's face? Or should they go to bed and enjoy a nice long sleep, undisturbed by the morning bell? They opted for sleep.

Sterling felt as if he had barely shut his eyes when he heard an annoying "clang, clang, clang." Was it a dream? Hadn't they silenced the bell? He rubbed his eyes. The clanging continued. It sounded as if it were coming from right outside his door. Sterling stepped into the hall. Other bleary-eyed students, awakened by the noise, stood at their doors, too.

They watched in amazement as the janitor marched down the hallway swinging a large dinner bell. "Up and at 'em," he said, smiling broadly as he passed each boy. "Clang, clang, clang," went the bell.

Despite his pranks, Sterling spent most of his time at the university studying. At that time the University of Michigan had 100 students, the biggest school Sterling had ever attended. Some of his classmates were very bright and dedicated scholars. In the past, Sterling had never had to try hard to stay ahead in his studies. But here, at the university, the competition was keen. Always an eager competitor, Sterling applied himself to schoolwork.

Literature and debate were his favorite subjects. He often wrote about studies in his diary: "Read all day nearly, and wrote some." "Up till midnight preparing for debate." "Read until three a.m."

He joined the debate team and served as the team's critic. He took his job seriously, listing detailed criticisms of the other debaters. No matter what topic the team debated, Sterling was ready with strong, persuasive arguments.

Students debated the issues of the mid-1800s. One of the most important was slavery. Should slavery be permitted in the new states being carved out of the western territories? The Compromise of 1850 made the question a hot topic. The law allowed California to enter the union as a free state. In other western territories waiting for statehood, the people there would vote free or slave. A special part of the compro-

In his junior year, Sterling was particularly proud of a literary project he started. Using his own money, he produced The Peninsular Quarterly and University Magazine. *It contained original stories and articles and several pages of advertising. Sterling's magazine was the first student publication in the university's history.*

mise was called the Fugitive Slave Law. It required people to return any runaway slave to the slave-holder.

The idea of carving new states out of the territories greatly attracted Sterling. At one debate he supported the resolution that "for every acre of federal land planted in trees, the government will give each planter three additional acres to use as his own."

Although no law existed which allowed for such an arrangement, Sterling thought it was a fine idea. He was glad for the chance to support it during the debate.

He rose to the stage. "Do we want growth?" Sterling asked the assembly. "Where nothing exists now, can we envision people, homes, livestock and farms? Much of the Great Plains is flat, dry land. In the future, will there be thick forests instead, as far as the eye can see? Yes, we possess land in abundance. But what we need are people to cultivate it, use it, better it."

When he sat down, the audience applauded. He liked this public display of approval. He especially liked the feeling that he had persuaded the crowd to his point of view.

When he first arrived in Ann Arbor, he promised himself that he would "keep straight" and do his best at school. And for the most part he did. Nevertheless, on May 5, 1854, six weeks before graduation, Sterling's university career suddenly ended. He was expelled.

Unusual events, as well as Sterling's own headstrong character, contributed to his expulsion. On May 4, one of the university's most popular professors was fired. He was Dr. Adams Allen, head of the school's medical department. Citizens of Ann Arbor and university students, especially Sterling, greatly admired Allen.

The night of the firing, a town meeting was called. It was a public protest of Allen's dismissal. During the meeting, the crowd began to shout, "Morton, Morton. Speak, speak."

No one knows for certain exactly what Sterling said when he took the podium. It is certain, however, that the seasoned debater who was known for his occasional hot temper did not speak kindly of the people who fired his friend. At any rate, the day after his speech, Sterling was expelled.

Within a few days, the entire state of Michigan was talking about the Allen controversy. Several articles were written about Sterling. The *Lansing Journal* criticized the school for expelling Sterling. The *Detroit Free Press* called Sterling "a worthy student friend" and described his "rare talents and gentlemanly deportment."

Sterling left Ann Arbor for Detroit where his parents had moved a year earlier. There he worked briefly as a reporter for the *Free Press*. The newspaper was run by Wilbur F. Storey, a fiery journalist who would one day become a famous editor. Storey believed newspapers were supposed to stir things up, and this appealed to Sterling.

Four years after Dr. Allen's firing, in 1858, the University of Michigan withdrew the expulsion and granted Sterling a degree. But by then he was hundreds of miles away.

By then, he had found his dream.

7

Bellevue

Despite the disappointments of college life, one thing remained true and certain: Caroline Joy French.

Sterling might be headstrong, but he was as steadfast as an oak tree. He said that he and Carrie would marry. He said that he would head for the territories when he finished school. The time had come for both.

Sterling picked the Nebraska Territory. This was an enormous land, stretching all the way to Canada. It included all of present-day Nebraska and Montana and portions of Wyoming, Colorado, North and South Dakotas. In May, 1854, Congress passed the Kansas-Nebraska Act which opened up more land for settlers. Sterling planned to be one of Nebraska's first settlers.

He was particularly interested in the little settlement of Bellevue on the territory's eastern

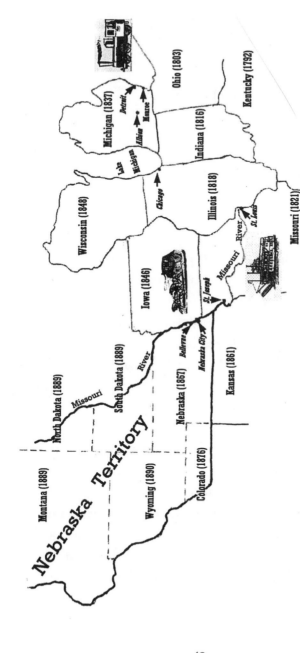

J. Sterling and Carrie Morton left Detroit for Nebraska Territory on the day they were married. They traveled more than 900 miles by train, boat and wagon to reach their new home in Bellevue, Nebraska.

48

edge. Some of Sterling's friends had already moved to Nebraska and lived near Bellevue.

At noon on October 30, 1854, Sterling and Carrie stood in the parlor of her adoptive parents. It was a small wedding. Only the two families attended. Shortly after the ceremony, the wedding party moved from the French home to the railroad depot. By early evening, the newlyweds were heading west toward Chicago.

From Chicago, they took a train to St. Louis. Here two great rivers converged: the Mississippi and the Missouri. It was the Missouri River which would take them into the country's vast frontier.

In the 1850s, the midwest from the Missouri River to the Rocky Mountains was sparsely populated. Easterners referred to this part of the country as the Great American Desert. They had no idea the land would one day become the nation's most important agricultural region. At that time it was largely an unmapped frontier, with no roads, no railroads or bridges, just a few wagon trails. The best way to travel into that "desert" was on a boat.

On the day Sterling and Carrie arrived in St. Louis, steamboats lined the levee. Most western travel occurred in the late spring and summer. But even now, in early November, wagons, freight and people filled the dock.

A steamboat carried about 400 to 500 passengers. The boats were beehives of humanity. There were soldiers and farmers, merchants and prospectors, preachers and gamblers, old trappers and newlyweds. Carrie wrote back home that many of the passengers on their boat, *New Lucy*, were children.

The Missouri River cut east/west across the state. Ten days after leaving St. Louis, *New Lucy* reached Kansas City. At that point the great river, called the Mighty Mo by many steamboat captains, turned abruptly north. Every year, the broad, turbulent river pulled one or more boats under its muddy waters.

But this year the river was low. When *New Lucy* reached St. Joseph, Missouri, the captain announced they could go no further. Sterling immediately set out to find an alternate route. He soon returned to Carrie with the news: a stagecoach would take them north.

Trains, boats and coaches. Sterling and Carrie had traveled every possible way. But after a journey of more than 900 miles, they still had

not reached their final destination. And yet they could see it.

The stagecoach dropped them off in St. Mary's, Iowa. Across the Missouri River was their new home, Bellevue, Nebraska.

It was the oldest permanent settlement in the Nebraska Territory. Although Native Americans had lived there for a long time, local settlers claimed that Manuel Lisa had given the place its present name, perhaps as early as 1807. Lisa was a fur trader. He dealt with native trappers all over the west. On horseback, on foot, and by boat, he traveled throughout the west to meet with Native Americans, buy their beaver furs, and ship those furs back to markets in the east. Sterling had heard that when Lisa first tried to travel on the Missouri River he complained that its muddy waters were too thick to drink, and too thin to plow!

Now that same river meant trouble for the newlyweds. Rough waters made the river crossing dangerous. No ferry owner was willing to take a chance. So Sterling and Carrie could only stare longingly at the far shore, and wait for calmer waters or a willing river man to take them over the churning Missouri River to the Nebraska side.

They waited three weeks. Finally a ferry transported them to the western shore. There they moved into a two-story log cabin. It stood on a high bluff, and the nearest neighbors, a band of Native Americans from the Omaha nation, lived on the flat riverbank below.

Sterling wasted no time getting to know other white settlers. Peter Sarpy had lived in the area for 30 years. He ran trading posts and was an agent for the American Fur Company. Judge Fenner Ferguson had recently been appointed Chief Justice of the Nebraska Territory. Thomas Morton (not related to Sterling) was the publisher of the *Nebraska Palladium*, the territory's first newspaper.

Like his new friends, Sterling was interested in seeing Bellevue prosper. Soon a territorial seat of government would be selected, and Sterling hoped to see Bellevue chosen. People in other, newly formed settlements were hoping the same thing for their towns. The town which was selected as the capital would become the center of commerce and political power in the territory. Bellevue, home to pioneers since the 1830s, was the logical choice.

That was the topic on everybody's mind during the winter of 1854. However, to everyone's surprise, on December 20, the Acting Governor of the territory selected a tiny hamlet 10 miles north of Bellevue, called Omaha. A ferry company in Council Bluffs, Iowa, had started Omaha. Its first cabin was built there on July 4, 1854, just a few months before its selection as the capital.

Sterling and his Bellevue neighbors were enraged. They claimed that the Acting Governor of Nebraska, who often stayed in Council Bluffs, had been influenced by Iowa businessmen. Sterling's Bellevue friends asked him to write an editorial against the Acting Governor's decision.

Sterling agreed. On January 3, 1855, the *Palladium* published his editorial. In it he asked for a "just government." He also called Tom Cuming, the Acting Governor, an "unprincipled knave" who was "neither an upright, honest nor honorable man."

A short time later, Sterling wrote another article in which he said, "The Indians have a name for me. They call me 'Tanu Geneka.' In English, it means 'Sleepy Buffalo Bull.' They call me this because they say I don't notice little irritations. But if you arouse my anger, I will come after you."

Sterling had been in Nebraska for less than four months. Already he had established himself as a leader...and a spirited fighter.

8

Nebraska City

 The decision about the territory's seat of government split the state in two: the north versus the south. The Platte River was the dividing line. Although Bellevue was north of the river (the same side as Omaha), it aligned itself with southern settlements.

Sterling wrote several articles for the *Palladium* against making Omaha the capital, and his strong opinions attracted widespread attention. He even suggested that the region south of the Platte River should become part of Kansas. The settlers in one of the southern towns asked Sterling to move to their town and work for their newspaper, the *Nebraska City News*.

Sterling believed in the power of the press. Like other settlers, he had come west to find fame and fortune. And he was convinced that if he could run his own newspaper, he could achieve both.

In April, 1855, Sterling and Carrie set out for Nebraska City, about 40 miles south of Bellevue.

Their new home was a river town, like Bellevue. A waterway, during the 1800s, was an ideal location. Since there were few roads and no railroads, the river was the best way to travel. Therefore, property in and around towns like Nebraska City soon became expensive.

Sterling and Carrie bought a quarter section (160 acres) of land just west of Nebraska City. Carrie then returned to Detroit for the summer. She was pregnant and wanted the comfort of a modern town for the birth of the baby. On September 27 Carrie gave birth to their first son who was given Carrie's maiden name: Joy.

While she was away, Sterling lived in a log cabin on their new property and oversaw the construction of their permanent home. Though small, it was the first frame house between the Missouri River and the Rocky Mountains. This house would one day become Arbor Lodge.

Life was busy for Sterling in 1855. Soon after Joy's birth, Nebraska City voters elected Sterling one of three representatives to the Territorial Legislature.

Nebraska was booming. Settlers streamed into the region. Land prices skyrocketed. To handle the increased financial activities, the

Joy Morton was Sterling and Carrie's oldest son. He grew up to become the owner of the internationally known Morton Salt Company. Inheriting his father's love of trees, Joy founded the Morton Arboretum west of Chicago, Illinois. He lived in and expanded Arbor Lodge after his father died.

Territorial Legislature passed a law creating several banks. The law didn't require these banks to maintain the usual reserve of money needed for future expenses. But the law did allow them to speculate — make risky business transactions — without any restrictions, such as requiring collateral (assets to back up a transaction).

Many people from Sterling's district praised the new banking law. Sterling hated it. He warned against speculation. He said all business transactions needed solid security. "It's impossible to create something from nothing," he said, adding that the law would cause Nebraska to commit "financial suicide."

When Sterling returned home after the legislative session, he found that his neighbors were angry with him. Why had he stood in the way of progress? What could possibly stop the boom? Everyone expected to become rich overnight. To provide for new businesses and settlers, buildings were going up night and day. Construction work was done by lamplight.

When Sterling ran for reelection the next year, he was soundly defeated. The speculators, who ran the "wildcat banks," continued operations for another year. And then a terrible thing happened.

A financial panic began to spread through the east, beginning when a huge business called the Ohio Life Insurance Company failed to pay its debts. In a short time, nearly 5,000 businesses failed. Eventually the economic uncertainty spread west to the frontier.

Within weeks, the Nebraska wildcat banks folded. These banks failed because they had no real assets — no "solid security," as Sterling had said. When the sheriff came to evict the operators of one bank, all he found were 13 bags of flour, an iron safe, three chairs, a counter, desk, stove and one map of the county.

Nebraskans struggled to recover from the economic chaos which followed the crash of the banks. And in their scramble to rebuild their lives and businesses, they remembered Sterling.

He had never wavered in his conviction about the wildcat banks. Like his grandfather, he was outspoken and stubborn. Week after week, month after month, he had written in the *Nebraska City News*, warning his readers about the dangers of unsound speculation.

People who had once turned against him now praised him. In the fall of 1857, they elected him once again to represent them at the Territorial Legislature.

9

Plant Trees!

Sterling's second election to the Territorial Legislature surprised him. He had almost given up on his political future in Nebraska. During the many months of the wild-cat banks, Sterling had written strong, critical articles in the *Nebraska City News* to fight the speculators. But the unpopularity of his writings had caused him to turn more and more attention to his new farm.

The farm was on a grassy hill west of Nebraska City. It sat high above the town between two Missouri River tributaries, North Table Creek and South Table Creek. Below, stately cottonwoods, oaks, and hickory trees lined the creeks.

On the day they bought the hilltop property, Sterling and Carrie drove up to the crest of the hill. "This is where we'll build the house," Carrie said.

Sterling nodded. Already in his mind, he could see their future home and the fields surrounding it.

They climbed from the buggy and looked out to the west. The Nebraska prairie, a sea of lush greens, spread out before them. This was Sterling's dream. This land, wide-open, untamed. It was like a blank piece of paper. He could write on it. Instead of words, he could use stones and timber for buildings. And he could use crops and orchards for harvests. And he could use flowers and vines for beauty. With a broad sweep of a brush, he could sign his name on this land. And it would matter. And if he were careful and fair and wise, it would matter for a long, long time.

Sterling remembered what people back east said about this territory. That it was the "Great American Desert." They said the land between the Missouri River and the Rocky Mountains was just a place to pass through on the way to the west coast. Nothing could grow on this harsh land, they said.

But Sterling strongly disagreed. He could see that the prairie was fertile, and he believed that Nebraska's future was agricultural. Sterling had wanted a working farm, and that's why he bought the property in Nebraska City. He would

This tall cottonwood tree is one of hundreds planted by the Mortons at Arbor Lodge in Nebraska City, Nebraska. J. Sterling Morton was particularly fond of cottonwoods which is the state tree.

raise hogs, sheep and cattle. He would plant corn, beans and grasses.

As the wildcat banks raced toward financial ruin, Sterling and Carrie began the first plantings on the farm. North of the house they put in a row of evergreen trees. In years to come this would provide a wind-break. He hired someone who owned oxen and a plow to till the ground.

Carrie, a skilled artist, drew a landscape design for the house and land. She sketched in vines, shrubs and flowers along the porch. Outside their bedroom window, she drew two apple trees. For the fields, she included berry bushes, ornamental trees and orchards.

When Carrie went to Detroit for the birth of their first son, Sterling accompanied her as far as St. Louis. There he bought several trees and had them shipped back to their Nebraska farm. Sterling mailed off orders to a nursery in Mt. Pleasant, Iowa, for seed packets and fruit trees.

⟫◆⟪

One day Sterling took a break from the newspaper and went to a nearby tavern to eat lunch. It was the summer of 1857. News of the financial disaster in the east hadn't yet reached the west. But that summer the west had a disaster of its own. Drought.

Many new settlers put all of their money and hopes into a fall harvest. After spring planting, the rains didn't come. The crops withered and died. By June the green prairies turned brown. Some settlers gave up. They packed their wagons and headed back east.

In the tavern, Sterling met one such settler.

"There's nothing out there," the man complained. "I've been half way across this territory, and it's flat as a skillet bottom. Not a tree for miles. But I found a nice little piece of land. Richest dirt I ever saw."

"Did you plant?" Sterling asked.

The man nodded. "I put in corn. Never saw a sprout. Without rain it was dead in the ground."

"But this is unusual weather," Sterling said. "We don't have a drought every year."

"It just takes one year," said the man.

And of course, the man was right. One bad year could wipe out an entire crop. Still, Sterling was sure something could be done to reduce the chances of losing an entire farm. Too little rain — or too much rain — in the spring could destroy corn, beans, grasses and any other field crop.

By the time Sterling returned to the newspaper office he had come up with an idea. He quickly wrote an article. When he finished, he had the typesetter spell out two words in large

letters for a headline. It read,

PLANT TREES!

The article under the bold headline urged people to set out a variety of trees. Shade trees. Flowering trees. Fruit trees. Hardwood trees. Once a tree is established, it is valuable for many years, sometimes for generations, Sterling wrote.

Trees provide food for the table, wood for the stove, shade for the body and beauty for the soul.

Sterling didn't know then that this would be his greatest legacy. Long after his political battles ended and were forgotten, his call to Plant Trees! would inspire people for more than a century.

An Important Citizen

W ildcat banks and drought weren't the only problems facing settlers.

The land which people moving into Nebraska claimed as their own actually belonged to someone else. The Pawnees. These Native Americans had lived on the prairie for hundreds of years. In 1857, the U.S. government asked the Pawnees to sign a treaty. The Pawnees agreed to turn over all their lands to the U.S. government. In exchange, the government promised to protect these Native Americans from their most feared enemies, the Sioux.

Several days before the treaty signing, the Pawnees gathered a short distance from the Morton house. Sterling and Carrie heard their singing and dancing as the tribe prepared for the big event.

The day before the signing, Gen. J.W.

Denver and other government officials arrived in Nebraska City. Gen. Denver spent the night at the Mortons' house.

Early the next morning, September 24, 1857, Sterling, Carrie and the representatives from the U.S. government walked down to the creek. There on the banks of the North Table, nine Pawnee chiefs and the U.S. officials signed the treaty.

When important events like the treaty signing occurred in Nebraska, Sterling was always invited. He was now one of the territory's most important citizens.

Although the 1857 drought discouraged some people, most settlers stayed in the territory, and more kept coming. Nebraska City grew daily. Sterling helped make the growth happen. His old newspaper, the *Detroit Free Press*, often carried his writings, as did other papers back east. Many of his articles, full of glowing reports about the opportunities in Nebraska, attracted readers as far away as Boston and New York.

Sterling's reports also impressed a man in Missouri. His name was Alexander Majors. Along with two partners, he owned the biggest wagon freighting company in the west.

As settlers moved across the Great Plains, the U.S. government built more and more military forts. The forts needed supplies, so the govern-

Alexander Majors, a wealthy freighter, was a friend of J. Sterling Morton. Majors' wagons and oxen hauled trading goods and military supplies throughout the American west. He also started the Pony Express and hired young, eager riders, including William Cody, later known as Buffalo Bill.

ment hired Majors' freighting company to ship goods to the western forts. The company operated from Kansas City, Missouri and Leavenworth, Kansas. But in 1858, Majors needed another huge staging area for his thousands of wagons and oxen. He traveled up to Nebraska City to talk with Sterling and other city leaders.

"How much land are you talking about?" Sterling asked.

He sat in the *Nebraska City News* office. The tall man across the desk held his hat in his lap.

Majors' trim mustache curled up on the ends. His black boots were polished and his hair was freshly combed. No one would guess that he had just ridden all the way from Missouri.

"Everything northwest of town," said Majors. "We'll need people, too. Bullwhackers, mule-skinners, teamsters, cooks, wagonmasters."

"I'll run an ad in the paper," Sterling assured him.

"We need as many as we can hire, but I don't want any troublemakers," said Majors. He was a soft-spoken man, but his voice was firm. "Every man who comes to work for me signs an agreement: no drinking, no gambling, no profane language. And any man I catch mistreating an animal is OUT. You put all that in your paper. I hire only gentlemen — and I pay good wages."

Sterling admired Majors. The freighter was Sterling's ideal of the western businessman. He had built a freighting empire on sound economic principles, not on speculation and risky business transactions.

Hardworking and honest, Majors had started out with only six wagons and a few oxen. He promised his clients "service, safety and speed." And he promised his employees "honesty and humane treatment." Within a few years, his company owned more than 3,000 wagons and 40,000 oxen. Majors eventually established a mail route,

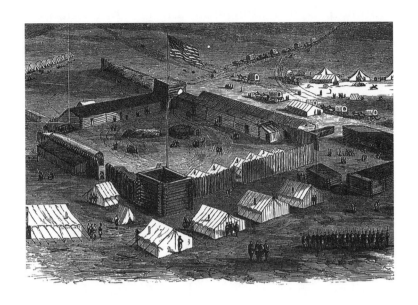

called the Pony Express. By then half a million people lived out west, and they needed a way to receive their mail.

Sitting in Sterling's office in the fall of 1858, Majors agreed to buy 138 lots in Nebraska City. His company would also construct a $300,000 warehouse in town.

One day, Sterling and Carrie stood on the hilltop of their farm. It was early morning. Toward the northwest, the first Majors' caravan was leaving. It was made up of 2,000 wagons hauling more than three million pounds of military supplies, the largest wagon train ever assembled. From first wagon to last, the caravan stretched 40 miles. All day long, the Mortons watched. By the afternoon, a long white ribbon of canvas-covered wagons extended as far as the eye could see.

"As far as the eye can see," Sterling said to himself. "As far as the *mind* can imagine." It was a land big enough to hold the dreams of a man like Alexander Majors — to hold the dreams of a man like J. Sterling Morton.

Sterling was less than 30 years old. In the four years since he and Carrie moved to the territory, he had watched the towns along the river grow from tiny outposts to booming communities. His own family had grown. He and Carrie now had three little boys: Joy, Paul and Mark.

The same year Majors came to town, Sterling received a letter from Washington, D.C. Would Julius Sterling Morton accept the position of Secretary of the Nebraska Territory? At the bottom of the letter was a signature:

*James Buchanan, President of the
United States of America.*

11

Mr. Secretary

Sterling accepted the position as Secretary of the Nebraska Territory. His appointment was immediately confirmed by the U.S. Senate. A few weeks later President Buchanan also appointed him Acting Governor of the territory. His new jobs took him to the capital in Omaha. Sterling soon discovered that being Secretary meant hard work.

One of his responsibilities was the capitol itself. The hastily constructed building was falling apart. Sterling wrote Congress in Washington, D.C., requesting money for repairs. He pointed out that the walls had separated from the foundation and "can only be secured by iron bolts passing through the building."

No repair money arrived. From time to time, fierce prairie winds tore out windows and doors. A large herd of cattle, which grazed nearby, wandered onto the capitol's yard and sometimes into the building itself. Sterling wrote Washington, D.C. again, this time asking for a fence around the building.

Other problems arose, too. Someone discovered gold along the lower South Platte River. Newspapers printed stories encouraging people to "Dig For Riches In Nebraska." Hopeful fortune-seekers invested all their money in prospecting equipment. When only a small amount of gold was found, fights broke out in towns along the river. Angry prospectors threatened to burn down the newspaper offices which had urged them to "Dig For Riches."

Around the same time, several Pawnees who had opposed the North Table Creek Treaty began raids against settlers in the territory. Sterling had to call in the militia to stop the attacks.

On a cold night in January, 1859, a gang of men broke into the Omaha jail. They dragged out two prisoners who had been arrested for horse stealing and drove them to Rockport, a few miles from Omaha. There the horse thieves were hanged from a tree. The lynch mob threatened violence against anyone who tried to punish members of the gang.

Not everything in the territory, however, was life-threatening. In September, 1859, Sterling's

This painting depicts the Table Creek Treaty signed by the Pawnee and the United States, represented by General J.W. Denver. In the 1857 treaty, the Pawnee gave up all their lands in the eastern Nebraska Territory. Sterling and Carrie attended the signing which occurred only a few miles north of the Morton farm. The painting now hangs at Arbor Lodge.

hometown, Nebraska City, hosted the first Territorial Fair ever held in the United States.

It was the territory's biggest event of the year. Businessmen showed the latest models in wagons, tillers and plows. Inventors exhibited newfangled gadgets: cherry pitters, treadle sewing machines and hair curlers. Ranchers marched their cows, pigs, horses and sheep past the judges' stands. Farmers displayed their fruits and vegetables. Children laughed at the clowns and gasped at the man who swallowed a sword.

Sterling, head of the territory, was a guest speaker. A large crowd gathered to hear him.

"We don't need to look for gold," he told the crowd. "It's right here. Tons of it. Under your feet."

The audience stared down at the ground.

"Do you see? The soil. That's our gold, our greatest wealth," he said. "But good soil can't last forever. It needs care and attention. We must sow and cultivate varieties of plants wherever they will take root. Fine young trees and healthy seeds can be brought to us by rail and by boat. But it's our duty to buy and plant them. If every farmer would set out a few forest trees, add a flower garden, and plant an orchard of fruit or nut trees, we would be an Eden on Earth, the envy of the east."

And then Sterling told the crowd something he had thought about ever since the last drought.

"If there is a crisis — if grasshoppers should eat our crops, if another drought should destroy our hard work — we may need some help. Let us form aid societies so families won't have to abandon their farms. These societies can make loans to help farm families recover from disaster. We don't need government to support our way of life. We will help each other in hard times."

He paused and looked out at the audience. "This is the Nebraska that I dream of — a land of abundance and generosity. Tell me, is that the Nebraska you dream of?" He waited while the people thought about his question.

"Yes!" someone called out.

"It is!" said another.

Soon shouts of agreement filled the fair-grounds.

"Then together, let's make that dream come true," he said, and sat down to loud cheers and clapping.

Sterling remained at the head of the territorial government for another year and a half. He might have had the job for another term but James Buchanan wasn't reelected president. Buchanan was unpopular. People in the west especially disliked him. He had vetoed the Homestead Act which would have given away 160 acres to anyone who lived on the land and worked it for five years. Settlers wanted free land. They agreed with Sterling that the soil and what the soil could produce with hard work was as good as gold.

A new president was now in Washington D.C. His name was Abraham Lincoln. In 1862, he would sign the Homestead Act into law. He would also appoint his own people to political positions such as the Secretary of the Nebraska Territory.

These were all issues which involved the west. But for President Lincoln, other parts of the country demanded his attention. The south and the north were pulling apart. Everyone feared a civil war.

12

Winning & Losing

Even before his term as Secretary of the Nebraska Territory ended, Sterling had thought about running for another political office. This time he would aim for a national position. He wanted to be the territory's delegate to the U.S. Congress.

Although settlers were interested in the presidential campaign of 1860, that election wasn't the biggest issue in the west. People in the territories couldn't vote for president. The Constitution only allowed citizens living in the states to do that. Those citizens could also vote for Senators and Representatives to Congress from their state. People in the territories could, however, vote for a delegate from their territory. And in 1860 that was the biggest issue: Who would win the election for delegate?

Sterling's opponent was Samuel Daily. Daily

was a member of Abraham Lincoln's political party, Republican. Sterling belonged to the opposing party, Democrat. That was also the party of the unpopular President Buchanan. As Buchanan's appointee, Sterling's name was linked to the president. Consequently, Sterling faced a fierce fight during the campaign for delegate.

Sterling had tried to do his best as Secretary. When he took over the office, he discovered that it owed $6,000. Three years later when he left office, it was debt free.

In 1860 voters relied on newspapers to learn about political issues and candidates. The *Nebraska City News* and other pro-Democrat newspapers carried articles praising Sterling. Pro-Republican papers like the *Nebraskan Advertiser* in Brownville supported his opponent, Daily.

Not everyone, however, received the newspapers. Most people in the territory lived outside the little towns. The 1860 election campaign was many years before radios and telephones. Political candidates had to travel around the countryside and talk directly to the people. A favorite method of attracting crowds of voters was to invite people to a series of debates between the candidates.

Therefore, in September Sterling and Sam

Daily rode all across the territory. They were on the road for several days at a time. Candidates had to pay most of their own expenses during a campaign. To save money, the two men traveled in the same buggy. Additionally, Sterling and Daily sometimes had to sleep in the same bed as it was often hard to find a place to spend the night on the sparsely populated frontier.

When they arrived at a settlement, the men would pass out leaflets inviting voters to come to the debate. People in the territory enjoyed these events. Political candidates brought news about what was happening in the government. Often living far from their neighbors, settlers welcomed the chance to socialize and express their opinions about life on the frontier.

At a debate, Sterling and Daily climbed on a wagon bed or stood on someone's front porch. The candidates sometimes talked for several hours. So people often brought picnic baskets.

Daily stood before the crowd. "I'm here to talk about freedom. Free men. Free land. Slavery should not spread to this territory. This is the land of free men. And I say, give these free men free land. There is plenty of land for every-one — if he is hardworking and honest." Daily pointed to Sterling. "This man is a Buchanan Democrat. He is against freedom. He would keep people in bondage. He would keep the land for the rich." Daily raised his fist dramatically over his head. "This election is about freedom!"

When the applause died down, Sterling stepped forward. "Bondage?" he asked the crowd. "Who here feels he is in bondage?" He paused a moment and then said, "I came to this great territory from the state of Michigan. Where are you from?"

"Indiana," a man on the front row said. Others called out: "Kentucky." "Ohio." "Pennsylvania." "Virginia." "New York." "Missouri." "Massachusetts." "Tennessee." Some people shouted foreign countries. "Scotland," one farmer said. "Austria." "Russia."

"I met a man from Missouri two years ago," said Sterling. "I'm sure you've heard of him. Alexander Majors. He started out as a dirt farmer. He now has the biggest freighting company in the country. After I moved to the Nebraska Territory, I built a house, I planted crops, I raised livestock. You, too, came to the territory and built a life for yourself. We all did this freely. The government didn't give these things to us. My opponent talks about 'hardworking and honest men.' I ask you, why does a hardworking and honest man need a government to give him anything? It is my deep belief that the less government interferes with our daily lives the better off we will be."

Once again the crowd applauded. Daily stood and responded to Sterling's speech. And then Sterling responded to Daily. Back and forth, it went as they traveled throughout the territory, repeating their speeches.

In towns along the river, one hundred or more people sometimes showed up for the debates. Out across the plains, Sterling and Daily often talked in front of a half a dozen or less voters.

It was a close election. When votes were tallied, J. Sterling Morton received 2,957 and Sam Daily, 2,943. Sterling won by only 14 votes.

Daily immediately called for a recount. He said there had been voter fraud and that he had won by more than 100 votes. He claimed ballots from pro-Republican counties had mysteriously disappeared. In some counties unqualified voters had cast ballots. Some voters had been bribed, he said.

Morton was indignant. He denied all charges. In fact, he made charges of fraud against Daily.

Before a delegate could formally represent the territory in the U.S. Congress, the Governor of the Territory, Samuel Black, had to sign certification papers. Governor Black assured Sterling that he would sign his papers. With that assurance and while the fight over voter fraud raged on, Sterling left for Washington, D.C.

When he arrived, he presented his papers to the House of Representatives. Unfortunately, Daily had arrived  first. He, too, had papers signed by Governor Black! The House could not seat both men, and Daily already had his name written on the House's official roll.

Congress was in no mood to listen to the squabbles of two would-be delegates from the territory. Members of Congress had more important things to worry about. On April 21, 1861, two and a half months before Sterling arrived in Washington, D.C., a Confederate cannon fired on Fort Sumter, a Union post in the Charleston, South Carolina harbor.

The Civil War had begun.

13

Civil War

Every year on his birthday, Sterling sent a letter to his mother, Emeline, who still lived in Detroit, Michigan. On April 22, 1861, he wrote her, "...I cannot write dreamily today nor well for I am cudgeling my poor brains nearly to death in the vain endeavor to find out some argument or scheme through, or by, which I shall secure my seat — to which I have been honestly elected."

Sterling stayed in Washington, D.C. for more than a year trying to secure his seat. He had no luck. Congressmen were not only busy with the war they also didn't want to seat a Democrat. The majority in Congress were members of the Republican party.

During the Civil War, it was hard to be a Democrat in the north. Most southerners were Democrats. And since the south had waged war

The Mortons' second son, Paul, started working for the railroads when he was only 16. He later became president of several companies. Paul served as Secretary of the Navy for his friend, President Theodore Roosevelt.

against the Union, many people in the north believed that all Democrats — southern *and* northern — hoped the Confederates would win. People said Sterling was a Copperhead, a southern sympathizer. Some even called him a traitor because he remained a Democrat during the war.

Even Julius Morton, Sterling's father, wrote his son about the dangers of remaining a Democrat. "I hope you will be a loyal citizen, supporting the Government right or wrong against the southern traitors & treason."

But Sterling, as always, was stubborn.

Of all the Morton's sons, Mark was the one most interested in farming. He received an honorary Doctor of Agriculture from the University of Nebraska in 1941. He also helped his brother, Joy, create the Morton Arboretum in Illinois.

Sterling was against the war because the war tore the country apart. Brothers fought brothers. Fathers fought sons. Sterling said that the Confederates were wrong to leave the union, but he couldn't side with the Republicans who continued to send armed soldiers into the south. President Lincoln said he wanted to preserve the Union. Sterling agreed the Union should be saved.

"But I don't believe," Sterling said, "that we can preserve the nation when we handle our disputes on the battlefield."

When Sterling returned home, he began writ-

89

ing articles and letters, trying to convince people to end the war. He called for compromise.

President Lincoln and others hoped the war would only last a few months. But the conflict raged for a year... then two years...then three. In 1864, more than half a million soldiers, north and south, were dead. That was nearly two percent of the nation's population. Sterling was very discouraged. For the first time in his life, he had grave doubts about the future of the nation.

In his 1864 birthday letter to his mother, Sterling wrote, "To me the future of what was once the United States looks dark and fearful, as a raging storm at midnight, when winds howl and torrents roar and danger shrieks in every blast."

While the war raged, Sterling spent more and more time at his farm. This was the place where he could always rally his spirits. At the darkest times in his life he could find comfort at the farm with Carrie and their sons.

That year he and Carrie ordered and planted hundreds of fruit trees. Even the three boys — Joy was now nine, Paul seven and Mark six — helped put the new additions in the ground. The orchard was growing and producing. Trees planted a few years earlier on the hilltop had grown so tall that they shielded the house from the strong winter winds, which swept up from

the prairie.

When the winter ended, wonderful news came with the spring of 1865. The war was over. The south surrendered on April 9 at Appomattox, Virginia.

The nation rejoiced.

A month earlier, during his second inaugural address, President Lincoln suspected that the end of the war was near. He asked his countrymen to devote all their strength to rebuilding the nation. He said, "With malice toward none, with charity for all...let us strive on to finish the work we are in, to bind up the nation's wounds, to care for him who shall have borne the battle and for his widow, and his orphan — to do all which may achieve and cherish a just and lasting peace among ourselves, and with all nations."

Six weeks after giving his speech, the president was assassinated. A nation which had rejoiced with the news of peace now wept in grief.

Like the rest of the country, Sterling was horrified at the crime. He had strongly disagreed with Lincoln about the war, but after Lincoln's death, Sterling never wrote another angry word against him. Lincoln's powerful voice was stilled, and Sterling would not criticize a man who could not answer.

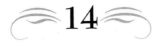

14

Statehood

A long time ago as a child, Sterling had stood in a sick room. His Aunt Mary lay on the bed near death. The room was dark. Members of his family gathered around the bed. Heads downcast, they whispered to each other. Sterling remembered the dark room and those whispers, sad and mournful. His family did everything possible to help Aunt Mary. They even cut her beautiful red hair in hopes of bringing some relief.

Finally, after what seemed an endless nightmare, Aunt Mary began to recover. Bit by bit her health improved. The curtains in her room were pulled back. Light returned. Life returned. Whispers became laughter.

Sterling thought about those bygone days. They reminded him of the endless war — "a raging storm at midnight, when winds howl and torrents roar and danger shrieks in every blast."

When the war finally ended it seemed that a black, heavy curtain had been lifted. Light returned. Life returned.

Life certainly returned to the Morton household when in early 1865 a fourth son was born to Sterling and Carrie. They named him Carl.

Sterling no longer feared for the future. He returned to his job as editor of the *Nebraska City News* with a revived spirit. As the U.S. government worked "to bind up the nation's wounds," as its fallen leader had urged, people in the territory began making plans for statehood.

Throughout the Nebraska Territory everybody talked about joining the union. In 1866 the territory's legislature gathered to vote yes or no on whether Nebraska should become a state. If the vote was yes then members of the legislature would write a state constitution. Voters of the territory would then approve or reject the constitution. This was a vote for or against statehood.

Admission, however, was a mutual agreement. In order for Nebraska to enter the Union, the people of the territory had to say they wanted to become a state, and the representatives of all the citizens of the United States— the Congress and the President — had to approve a bill admitting the territory into the union.

Sterling knew that Nebraska would eventually become a state. But he hoped to delay statehood until post-war problems were resolved. The war had ended and the killing had stopped, but what changes were in store for the country now that the south lay in ruins? What would happen to the country now that President Lincoln was dead?

As usual Sterling wasn't timid about expressing his concerns. He wrote strong articles against statehood in the *News*. The debate about Nebraska becoming a state reached a fever pitch. Pro-state newspapers once again called Sterling a Copperhead and a traitor. One man, a former officer in the Union Army, challenged Sterling to a duel.

Sterling said that the idea of a physical fight instead of a debate was ridiculous. He answered the man's challenge in a witty open letter published in the *News*. "...His proposition to shoot lead bullets at me is not in accordance either with law or my own ideas of social amenities and amusements...To kill or to be killed would be no particular felicity to me, especially in hot weather when corpses spoil so rapidly..."

By the 1860s settlements had sprung up all over the territory, not just along the river. The people living in the settlements wanted statehood. They wanted equal representation in

Washington, D.C. Even Nevada, which had hardly any people compared to Nebraska, was already a state.

Sterling listened to the pro-state arguments and then he did something he rarely ever did — he changed his mind. He decided that, under the wise leadership of President Andrew Johnson, the nation was recovering satisfactorily from the war. Early statehood, Sterling decided, was a good idea.

Sterling was certain voters would approve the constitution and statehood. At the same time people voted on the constitution, they would also elect candidates to represent them. Sterling hoped to be among the leaders of the new state. When the Nebraska Democrat party asked him to run for governor, Sterling accepted. He was also nominated to run for Senator to Congress, in case Nebraska was admitted to the union.

Once again Sterling was on the campaign trail. He traveled all over the territory, speaking in every town and hamlet. He stopped to talk to farmers and ranchers. Friends and enemies admired his speaking ability. He was Nebraska's best political entertainer, one newspaper said.

Ever since his university days, Sterling had loved to debate. He liked the chance to persuade people, to bring a crowd to his point of view. Sometimes he could make people agree with

Carl Morton was the fourth and youngest son of Sterling and Carrie. He was the founder of Argo Starch Works.

him. But opposition never stopped him. In fact, Carrie often said that opposition simply fueled his passion to fight harder than before.

Opposition against his ideas, however, was strong on election day in 1866. Sterling lost.

But voters did approve statehood. The following spring, on March 1, 1867, President Johnson proclaimed Nebraska the 37th state in the union.

Sterling celebrated with other Nebraskans. During the festivities, he had time to reflect on his political life. He was 36 years old. He was considered one of the "old men" of Nebraska politics. Much of the 13 years he had lived in the territory had been spent away from home. During his career, he had not only ventured across the Great Plains, he had also traveled to every major city in the east. He was often gone for months at a time. Writing, speaking, traveling — all to persuade people to his point of view.

For years Carrie had pleaded with him to stay home more. His boys were growing up. Every year they added new livestock, expanded the garden and planted trees. But Sterling was hardly ever there to enjoy them.

From the hilltop where his house stood, Sterling looked down at fireworks exploding over Nebraska City. "It's time to be home," he said to himself.

And so for the next 12 years he would be simply J. Sterling Morton. Husband, father, farmer. Private citizen of the great state of Nebraska.

15

Arbor Day

Carrie was often left to run the farm by herself because Sterling's work took him away from home. Nevertheless, he was deeply involved in the farm work, especially in tree planting. He set out hundreds of trees. He and his sons often worked side by side. One year, one thousand apple trees were added to the orchard. Sterling did much of the work himself. He trimmed and grafted favorite specimens.

Sterling loved all aspects of farming, but his favorite was tree cultivation. Through the years, he continued to urge people to "Plant Trees!" Forest trees were as important as fruit trees, Sterling believed. If everyone would plant just one tree a year, the Great Plains would become a vast, lush garden.

Just one tree a year, thought Sterling. And then it came to him. Why not have an annual

*After visiting Arbor Lodge in 1866, a
friend wrote, Sterling's "orchards, num-
bering hundreds of apple trees, remind
one of those a century old in the
East...All around that splendid farm
may be seen proof of the constancy with
which Mr. Morton has given direction to
fruit and tree culture. He is constantly
sticking the `cutting' or roots of fruit or
forest trees into the ground."*

event — an Arbor Day! On that day everyone
would plant a tree.

In 1872, at a meeting of the State Board of
Agriculture where he served as president,
Sterling announced his idea.

"Will it be like a club," someone asked, "and
each member plants a tree?"

"No, this is for everyone," said Sterling.

Some board members favored the name
"Sylvan Day," but others said that would apply
just to forest and shade trees. Some wanted only
orchard trees included. "Cottonwoods use up
good soil," one member complained. Some said
that tree planting was only possible in the eastern part of the state. Nothing would grow out
west, they said.

Sterling refused to waver. "This is for everybody," he said. "And no tree is more important
than another. I want us to get the word out to

everyone in this state. If every person plants just one tree on Arbor Day, Nebraska will have hundreds — thousands! — of new trees by sundown."

Finally everyone agreed. Arbor Day would be open to all people and to all types of trees. To encourage participation, Sterling suggested that county agricultural groups compete for a $100 prize. The person who planted the most trees would win $25 worth of farming books.

The first Arbor Day was April 10, 1872. Even if the little seedling was only a few inches high, Sterling said it would one day shade a house, produce a bushel of nuts or fruit, or provide wood for a cold winter night. Sterling was astonished at its success and popularity. Everyone — children and adults, farmers and town residents, rich and poor — put a tree in the ground. On that first Arbor Day, Nebraskans planted one million trees!

The next year the U.S. Congress passed the Timber Culture Act. It extended the Homestead Act and allowed settlers to claim an additional 160-acre tract if they planted 40 acres of it in trees.

Sterling's great idea continued. In 1885, in honor of Sterling's birthday, Arbor Day was moved to April 22. Twenty years after the first Arbor Day, Nebraska had added six million more trees to the land. By then the tradition had spread to other states.

(Left) Through the years the Mortons remodeled their home, Arbor Lodge. The top photograph shows the house around 1860. It was the first frame house between the Missouri River and the Rocky Mountains. The remodeled house in the middle was completed in 1879, in time for Sterling and Carrie's 25th wedding anniversary. The third house was finished about 1890, two years before Sterling became U.S. Secretary of Agriculture.

Sterling had not been successful in politics. But he always believed in the central promise of American democracy: that all people have a right to be treated equally under the law. On the first Arbor Day, Sterling wrote an article for the *Omaha Daily Herald*. In it he talked about how trees honor democracy:

> *There is no aristocracy in trees. They are not haughty. They will thrive near the humblest cabin on our fertile prairies...and become just as refreshing to the eye and as fruitful as they will in the shadow of a king's palace.*
>
> *The wealthiest and most powerful potentate on earth cannot hire one to speed its growth or bear fruit before its time. There is a true triumph in the unswerving integrity and genuine democracy of trees, for they refuse to be influenced by money or social position.*

16

Rails West and East

A few months after statehood celebrations, Nebraska City held a gala in honor of Alexander Majors. Sterling, a close friend of the famous freight company owner, gave a speech. He praised Majors for helping to open the west to commerce and settlers.

Without the thousands of wagons and the tons of freight hauled by Majors' company, the west would have remained a frontier. Sterling knew this. But he also knew that by the time the Civil War ended a new form of transportation was overtaking the covered wagons.

The railroad was coming. Already the race was on to connect the eastern edge of the territory with the far west. A rail line across the Great Plains and over the Rocky Mountains would cost an enormous amount of time and money. It also would require back-breaking work. That work began during the Civil War. On May 10, 1869, the connecting railroad was finally complete. It ran from Omaha, Nebraska, to Sacramento, California.

Sterling understood the importance of the western connection. The rail line would help move settlers and their belongings to the frontier. But Sterling was a farmer; his region, the Great Plains, was agricultural. How would he and his neighbors get their crops and cattle to *eastern* markets? The old way, by boat and wagon, was much too slow.

Sterling wanted an eastern connection. He wanted to link the Great Plains with the major markets in the east — St. Louis, Chicago, Boston, Philadelphia and Baltimore. In the mid-1860s the best and fastest way to link cities was the locomotive.

Several rail companies also wanted to hook up the east to the west. Since they had their main offices in the east, the companies needed someone who knew the west and who understood the needs of settlers. That someone was J. Sterling Morton. For many years after he quit politics, Sterling worked for the railroad companies.

Although he worked for the railroads, his passion was still his farm. Compared to the frustrations and defeats of politics, the glory of

bountiful trees warmed Sterling's heart. Sterling loved taking guests on a tour of his orchards. In spring the rows of blossoming trees filled the air with their fragrance. At harvest time hundreds of trees produced apples, peaches, plums and pears.

Sterling not only planted trees, he experimented with different varieties. One of his visitors wrote that "he is constantly sticking the 'cuttings' or roots of fruit or forest trees into the ground. When he is not doing this, in the proper season he is using a pair of shears ingeniously fastened on a long pole and operated with a string, in trimming the limbs of the tall trees."

At the first Territorial Fair, Sterling had told people that the prairie earth was like a gold mine. Now there were State Fairs. Every year people had a chance to show off the harvests from that gold mine. And what a dazzling display! Every kind of vegetable, grain and fruit. The finest livestock — from saddle horses to draft oxen. There wasn't much scientific information then. People learned by trial and error. The fairs also gave people like Sterling the chance to share what they had learned about farming.

Getting the word out about farming wasn't just meant for people living on the frontier. Sterling wanted people in the east to know about western agriculture, too. Although every day brought new settlers to the frontier, there were still people who believed that the country west of the Missouri River was a desert. Nothing but buffalo and sagebrush could live out there, they believed. Sterling remembered that as a young boy living in Michigan he had seen a map which called the prairie the Great American Desert. He was amazed that people still believed that.

During the 1873 State Fair, Sterling and some other farmers had an idea. Why not take the best fruits and vegetables back east and show the people there the glories of a prairie harvest?

Governor Robert Furnas, Morton's friend and one of the state's most successful farmers, agreed. "We could certainly change some minds." Governor Furnas nodded to the long rows of colorfully displayed produce. "But how can we haul ripe fruit 1,300 miles in the heat of

J. Sterling Morton was editor of one of Nebraska Territory's earliest newspapers. Just before the Civil War, between 1858-1861, he served as the territory's secretary and governor.

summer without it rotting? I don't think we would impress many people with a mountain of stinking produce."

"We'll take it by rail," said Sterling. "That's the only way it can be done."

"Too expensive," said Furnas. "Rail would speed the journey, but who'll pay for it? The

State Board of Agriculture can't afford it."

Luckily Sterling worked for a railroad company which agreed to pay for the entire trip. Railroad officials even authorized the construction of a special rail car to transport the produce. In September, right after the fair ended, the special car was loaded with 237 varieties of apples; 49 of pears; 25 of peaches; 14 of grapes; three of plums and 12 of evergreens.

That day Governor Furnas, Sterling and his son, Joy, left Lincoln for the east coast. At every city, the railroad company telegraphed ahead an announcement about the arrival of the Nebraska "Car of Fruit." The train traveled to Burlington, Iowa, then to Chicago, Illinois and then to Boston, Massachusetts. It stopped in Boston long enough for them to enter the Nebraska produce in the competition at the American Pomological Society. [Pomology is the study and cultivation of fruit.]

The Nebraska exhibit won first place for the best collection of apples and a medal for its pears. Peaches, plums and grapes won honorable mention.

Sterling and the Nebraska delegation took the special car on to New York City where Nebraska's agricultural triumphs again were displayed. So successful was the tour that everyone decided to send the fruit collection on to

London, England.

Sterling was proud of Nebraska's showing in the east. He knew the trip's success was more than winning a few medals and first-place ribbons. Newspapers from Burlington to New York — even London — sang the praises of western agriculture. Now people knew that the west was not a Great American Desert.

17

Laughter & Tears

Twenty five years. That's how long Sterling and Carrie had been married, from 1854 to 1879. They had also lived in the west for 25 years.

"Twenty five years!" said Carl, their youngest son. "A quarter of a century! That's forever!" He was 14 years old and the last Morton son still living at home. Joy, Paul and Mark now had households of their own. Joy lived in Omaha. Paul and Mark lived in Chicago.

"And just think, Sterling and I were betrothed for seven years before we were married," said Carrie. She sat at her easel, sketching the two apple trees she and Sterling had planted by the house when they first moved to the hilltop. That was almost 25 years ago, too. The two trees now stood as tall as the house. "So that means your father and I have known each other for 32 years."

This is Arbor Lodge today. Along with the expansive grounds, it is a Nebraska state park. After J. Sterling Morton died, his son, Joy, lived in the house and later donated it to the state.

"That's twice as old as me," Carl said in wide-eyed wonder.

"As `I'," corrected Sterling. "'Twice as old as I'."

"Did you know Manuel Lisa?" Carl asked his father excitedly. "Did you go with Lewis and Clark on the Corps of Discovery?"

"Let's see," said Sterling, as if pondering a math problem in his head. "If I'd been old enough to go on the Lewis and Clark expedition in 1803, I would be about 100 years old now. Do you think I'm 100 years old?"

"If you're 100 years old," teased Carl, "we should have a party."

Carrie turned from her drawing. "That's a wonderful idea. We'll have a silver anniversary party."

Sterling thought it was a great idea, too. The party would celebrate their long life and happy home together. The family called their home Arbor Lodge.

During their 25 years together, Sterling and Carrie had known many hard times. Carrie remembered one bitterly cold winter night when the houseplants froze and the ink turned to ice in the bottle. She wrote, "If I live another winter in this country I shall have two or three coal stoves and not fuss with wood every five minutes."

And there was the year grasshoppers invaded the prairie. The 1875 attack was the worst in living memory. The insects swept over the land like a black cloud. Entire counties suffered from the infestation. Sterling wrote in his farm journal, "Where they lighted they covered the ground like a heavy crawling carpet. Growing crops disappeared in a single day."

It was true that Sterling and Carrie had known bad times. But those hardships simply served to highlight the joys. And the greatest joys were their boys.

A proud father, Sterling wrote his mother, "Few fathers have been awarded such a quadruple blessing of Boys and no parents ever had less anxiety or shed fewer tears over sons. Each one is truthful, honest, industrious and all of pride-of-good-name...They will do better than I have, and will establish a family name of which we shall all be proud."

And being so proud of his family, the idea of an anniversary party was particularly pleasing. Sterling wanted Arbor Lodge in tiptop shape for the gala. With suggestions from Carrie, he planned major remodeling of the house. By summer, Sterling wrote, the family was living "among paper-hangers, carpenters, plasterers, plumbers, and general noise makers." He also planted 1,175 trees.

When remodeling was finished, the *Nebraska City News* reported about Arbor Lodge, "Lighted up by the shimmering glory of a Nebraska sunset, there is no place west of the Hudson River and this side of California that can compare with it."

Two hundred fifty people attended the anniversary party in October. They danced to the music of an orchestra from Omaha. Lanterns decorated the house and grounds. After sunset, the candlelight glittered and the whole night seemed touched by magic.

At midnight, a huge banquet was served. In the middle of the table, surrounded by bouquets of flowers, stood a tall silver cup. Sterling had this loving cup made especially for this evening. Inscribed on the cup were the six names of the

Mortons and these words:

By our lives we will honor this home, and perpetuate the good name of its founders.

Of all the nights of his life, Sterling would remember this one as the best. He watched his wife and boys laugh and spin around the dance floor. The next day, he wrote his sister, Emma, about the party,

The Mother and the sons whirled around and around, laughing and talking, while all the guests admired, and an old fellow, who will sign this letter, sat off in a corner and, very quietly, wiped warm tears of gladness out of his gratified eyes... Altogether the affair was satisfactory and illustrated the fact that after a quarter of a century in Nebraska we still have friends and still enjoy life...

That was the last big party Sterling and Carrie would share at Arbor Lodge. The next year, Carrie fell as she stepped from a carriage. Although she didn't realize it at the time, the fall had injured her critically. After many months of terrible pain, Carrie died on June 29, 1881. The whole town mourned. Not one Nebraska City business opened its door. Not one person went out of the house except to attend the graveside service. The sons who had danced so gaily with her on that magic anniversary night now carried

117

her casket to the grave.

Sterling could not be consoled. For months he remained isolated. He visited Carrie's grave every day. He designed a special memorial to be carved in her honor.

Once upon a time he had a dream about building a life on the frontier of the American West. What would he do now that part of the dream was gone?

18

U.S. Secretary of Agriculture

Sterling was slow to recover from Carrie's death and to find some meaningful work. For the most part, his work had centered on life in the American West. Nevertheless, his contributions to farming had gained national attention, especially his call to "Plant Trees!" He had been elected president of the American Forestry Association. Twenty years after Sterling started Arbor Day, the annual tree planting became a tradition in many states.

In 1893 Grover Cleveland was elected president for the second time. When he needed to select someone as his Secretary of Agriculture, he looked to the west. By then, thanks to people like J. Sterling Morton, the country no longer thought of the nation's heartland as a desert, but as a strong agricultural region.

On February 15, while visiting his sons in

Chicago, Sterling received a telegram:

J. STERLING MORTON - CAN YOU
MEET ME AT LAKEWOOD, NEW JERSEY
AND HOW SOON
- GROVER CLEVELAND.

Sterling was very surprised. For several years, he had strongly criticized some of Cleveland's political decisions. Even so, the president felt that no other person in the country could do the secretary's job better than Sterling.

Along with his son, Paul, Sterling traveled to New Jersey, where he accepted the position. His appointment as Secretary of Agriculture was history-making. Sterling was the first man from west of the Missouri River to serve on a president's cabinet.

Newspapers praised the choice. The *Louisville Courier Journal* said, "If the President had raked the party with a fine-tooth comb he could not have found a Democrat so fitted in all points for this important post." The *Kansas City Star* said, "No better appointment has been made by any President."

All four of Sterling's sons and their wives traveled with him to Washington, D.C. where he was sworn into office. His sister, Emma, remained in Washington with him. The two lived

J. Sterling Morton's statue, by Rudulph Evans, is in Washington, D.C.'s Hall of Fame.

in a small apartment. She served as hostess and accompanied him to important official events.

Being a cabinet member was certainly a great honor. But Sterling didn't let the importance or pressures of the office change the things he had always believed. He was the same man in Washington as he had been all his life — stubborn and outspoken. He was still the man who had fought the wildcat banks and who believed in thrift and careful management of resources.

And so Sterling set about to streamline the Department of Agriculture. One thing that bothered him was the time-honored practice of giving government jobs to friends and family members. These people weren't always good workers, and the jobs they held weren't always necessary. Sterling wanted to eliminate unnecessary jobs. He also wanted a system of hiring only qualified people who would be promoted because of their skills and dependability.

When Sterling was secretary, many Department of Agriculture workers went on trips paid for by the government. Sterling stopped this practice. He also refused to pay for any government program which only helped a few people. "Government," he said, "should serve the public good, not a handful of private citizens."

He sent out a letter announcing his intentions. "I wish it distinctly understood that wherever there is an opportunity to economize, it should be embraced with alacrity, and that if you do not economize someone will be put in your place who will."

Many people criticized Sterling. They said he was trying to change a long- respected system. They also believed that sometimes it was important to help people — even if only a few people — who might not be able to help themselves.

Sterling said no. "Tax money raised by all the people," he said, "should not be spent on a few."

These were important matters. They had

Rudulph Evans is working on the statue of J. Sterling Morton. Evans, who became a famous artist, received early encouragement from Sterling who recognized the young man's talent. Evans made both the Morton statue in Washington, D.C. and the one at Arbor Lodge. With pennies, nickels and dimes, children across the world helped pay for the one in Nebraska.

always been debated in politics, and they would continue to be debated. But while Sterling was Secretary of Agriculture he was determined to be thrifty.

And he was. Sterling was secretary for four years. His department's budget was $11,179,445.45. When he left office, after Cleveland's presidency was over, Sterling returned to the national treasury $2,066,661.19.

Sterling could be stubborn in his views about thrift. But he never lost his sense of humor. In a speech about the problems of taxes, he told a story about a farmer.

"You see," Sterling said, "the farmer wakes up very early in the day. He eats a good breakfast. He spends the day working in the fields. In the evening he puts the draft animals away in the barn and washes up for supper. He kisses his wife and children, puts on his nightclothes, and falls fast asleep. And the only thing the government doesn't tax is his snoring."

Certainly Sterling had many critics. But he also had fans. In fact, toward the end of Cleveland's term in office, there was talk about Sterling running for the presidency. Sterling said no. He would never again run for political office. He was too old, he said. Other young people were starting to make a name for themselves, including another Nebraskan named William Jennings Bryan.

"I'm going home to run my farm," he said, as he prepared to leave Washington, D.C. "I'm heading west."

19

He Was a Tree

What now?" Sterling thought. The passenger train clattered along, hurrying west toward Nebraska and Arbor Lodge. "I can't just go home and sit in an easy chair, staring into the fireplace."

He spread a newspaper across his lap, thinking that a bit of reading would quiet his rushing thoughts. Then it came to him.

A newspaper. He would end his working life the same way it began. He remembered his Uncle Edward and the *Monroe Advocate*. It seemed so long ago. How he had loved to sit in the *Advocate* office! Even now he could almost smell the ink and hear those fiery debates.

Yes, he would launch a newspaper. In it he would express his political views. He would share his knowledge about farming. And he would encourage people to Plant Trees!

He called his newspaper *The Conservative*. In one editorial he wrote, "When I came to Nebraska Territory, it was barren, treeless, and plain. Every new tree has done its part to beautify our home state, to preserve and strengthen the soil. Trees have given us wealth, but most of all a heartfelt joy."

———◆———

A few years later, another article in another newspaper had this to say:

He was a tree, sturdy and deep-rooted, able to withstand bad weather. We are a tree-conscious country because of him. If something was lacking in nature, he knew that Nature was only waiting for man to help out. Wherever things would grow, it was man's duty to plant something there.

He made a study of soil, streams, and forests. As he came to know and love the natural world, he came to know and love us, too.

This article was written shortly after Sterling's death. It was 1902, five days after his 70th birthday. He was in Lake Forest, Illinois, at his son Mark's, home. He had been ill for several months.

Hundreds of people turned out in Nebraska City when the train carrying his body pulled in from Chicago. He had once again made that long journey west to the land of his dreams.

Sterling was remembered by the entire nation, at that time 45 states. Within a few years, several statues were erected in his honor. He would have appreciated these kind gestures. But he really didn't need memorials. His real memorials — trees — were already in place, growing and thriving all around the world. They were tall and short, food-bearing or simply pretty. They might be used, or they might be left alone to be admired.

Trees are his legacy.

Like most great ideas, Arbor Day refused to fade away. The United States had once had forests almost from coast to coast. Trees were cleared out to make room for crops and housing. Now it was time to restore some of the lost woodlands.

Within 20 years of the first Arbor Day all but one state took part in the annual tree planting event. Foreign countries had their own Arbor Days. Children of Great Britain planted trees. African children recited poems about trees as they put them in the ground. French children did a dance to honor trees. In Japan, Canada, Austria and Hungary children worked on essays for Arbor Day competitions.

A resolution of the United States Congress

This is a 1932 Arbor Day stamp, which celebrated the 60th anniversary of the first Arbor Day.

created a National Arbor Day, to be held on the last Friday of April. This is the only national observance which honors the future rather than the past. Due to the various growing cycles in different climates, Arbor Day is now celebrated at different times. It varies from mid-January in Louisiana to May in North Dakota. Hawaiians plant their trees in November.

Because of increasing concern for the earth, its forests and its atmosphere, Arbor Day is more important than ever. In most states, the local departments of conservation are involved.

Betty Morton, J. Sterling Morton's great grand-daughter, is buying Arbor Day stamps in Nebraska City, Nebraska.

They provide seedlings on request, give workshops on pruning and grafting, and visit schools to help with planting.

Chicago started a model program. Money raised by bake sales was invested in honey locust trees. In just two years, one group planted 800 trees on vacant lots. Another student group raised funds to bring a six-foot sapling to their neighborhood. This sapling is the "child" of a tree in Lithuania. The parent tree is 30 feet wide, and thought to be 2000 years old.

One year, Wisconsin's governor appealed to

the citizens for help replacing trees lost to a drought and fire. A seventh grade class put 5,000 seedlings in the burnt-out area.

Children in Pennsylvania wanted to honor other children who had died from illness, abuse or neglect. Every tree planted had a ribbon and memorial name tag.

All this happened because of J. Sterling Morton. His love of nature was his gift to all humankind. As a little boy he helped two home-less birds. As a man, Sterling started Arbor Day and helped the world.

Sandy Beaty has been involved with books for two decades. She lives in Kansas City, Missouri where she works at the University of Missouri at Kansas City's Miller Nichols Library. A former English teacher, she also owns one of Kansas City's oldest and best-known bookstores, the Book Shop in Brookside. This is her first book for children.

J.L. Wilkerson, a native of Kentucky, now lives in Kansas City, Missouri. A former teacher, Wilkerson has worked as a writer and editor for more than 20 years. She is an award-winning writer whose essays and articles have appeared in professional journals and popular magazines in the United States and Great Britain. She is the author of several regional history books, including *Path To Glory: A Pictorial Celebration of the Santa Fe Trail*. Wilkerson also is the author of three children's books.

Order Form

Mail orders to: Acorn Books,
The Great Heartlanders Series,
7337 Terrace
Kansas City, MO 64114-1256

☐ Please send an Acorn Books catalog for a complete listing of biographies and educational materials from The Great Heartlanders Series

☐ Please send the following books and activities: I understand that I may return any books for a full refund.

Scribe of the Great Plains: Mari Sandoz
    ☐ One book @ $8.95
    ☐ Five books @ $37.50
    ☐ Ten books @ $73.00

Champion of Arbor Day: J. Sterling Morton
    ☐ One book @ $8.95
    ☐ Five books @ $37.50
    ☐ Ten books @ $73.00

☐ Fun Activities for *Scribe of the Great Plains* @ 12.95
☐ Fun Activities for *Champion of Arbor Day* @ $12.95

Add 10% of total for shipping: _____
Missouri add sales tax: _____
TOTAL: _____

Make checks payable to Acorn Books.

Please send to:
Name: _____
Address: _____
City:_____ State: ____ Zip Code: _____
Telephone: _____ E-Mail: _____

Thank you for your order!

Order Form

Mail orders to: Acorn Books,
                    The Great Heartlanders Series,
                    7337 Terrace
                    Kansas City, MO 64114-1256

☐ Please send an Acorn Books catalog for a complete
   listing of biographies and educational materials
   from The Great Heartlanders Series

☐ Please send the following books and activities:
   I understand that I may return any books for a full
   refund.

Scribe of the Great Plains: Mari Sandoz
   ☐ One book @ $8.95
   ☐ Five books @ $37.50
   ☐ Ten books @ $73.00

Champion of Arbor Day: J. Sterling Morton
   ☐ One book @ $8.95
   ☐ Five books @ $37.50
   ☐ Ten books @ $73.00

☐ Fun Activities for *Scribe of the Great Plains* @ 12.95
☐ Fun Activities for *Champion of Arbor Day* @ $12.95

Add 10% of total for shipping:
Missouri add sales tax:
TOTAL:

Make checks payable to Acorn Books.

Please send to:
Name: _____
Address: _____
City:_____ State: ____ Zip Code: _____
Telephone: _____ E-Mail: _____

Thank you for your order!

Order Form

Mail orders to: Acorn Books,
                      The Great Heartlanders Series,
                      7337 Terrace
                      Kansas City, MO 64114-1256

☐ Please send an Acorn Books catalog for a complete
    listing of biographies and educational materials
    from The Great Heartlanders Series

☐ Please send the following books and activities:
    I understand that I may return any books for a full
    refund.

Scribe of the Great Plains: Mari Sandoz
    ☐ One book @ $8.95
    ☐ Five books @ $37.50
    ☐ Ten books @ $73.00

Champion of Arbor Day: J. Sterling Morton
    ☐ One book @ $8.95
    ☐ Five books @ $37.50
    ☐ Ten books @ $73.00

☐ Fun Activities for *Scribe of the Great Plains* @ 12.95
☐ Fun Activities for *Champion of Arbor Day* @ $12.95

Add 10% of total for shipping:
Missouri add sales tax:
TOTAL:

Make checks payable to Acorn Books.

Please send to:
Name: _____
Address: _____
City:_____ State: ____ Zip Code: _____
Telephone: _____ E-Mail: _____

Thank you for your order!